what do

Pulleys and

Gears

do?

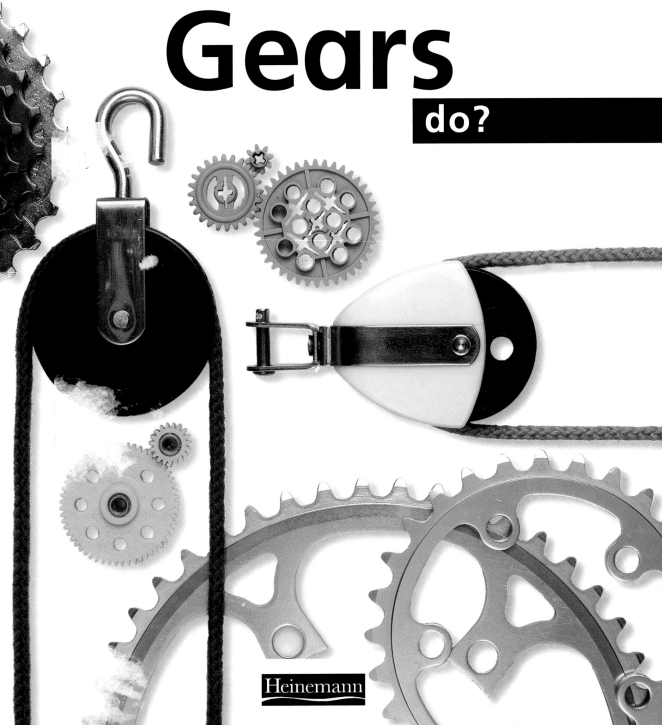

Heinemann

David Glover

First published in Great Britain by Heinemann Library
Halley Court, Jordan Hill, Oxford OX2 8EJ
a division of Reed Educational & Professional Publishing Ltd.

MELBOURNE AUCKLAND
FLORENCE PRAGUE MADRID ATHENS
SINGAPORE TOKYO SÃO PAULO
CHICAGO PORTSMOUTH NH MEXICO
IBADAN GABORONE JOHANNESBURG
KAMPALA NAIROBI

Designed by Celia Floyd and Sharon Rudd
Illustrated by Barry Atkinson (pp8, 9, 11, 17) and Tony Kenyon (p7)
Printed in Hong Kong / China

01
10 9 8 7 6 5 4
ISBN 0 431 06272 2

British Library Cataloguing in Publication Data

Glover, David
    What do pulleys and gears do?
    1. Pulleys – Juvenile literature 2. Gearing –
    Juvenile literature
    I. Title II. Pulleys and gears
    621.8 ' 3

Acknowledgements

The Publishers would like to thank the following for permission to reproduce photographs:
Trevor Clifford pp4, 5, 12, 14–19, 21, 23; Collections/Keith Pritchard p9; Mary Evans Picture Library p10; Stockfile/Steven Behr p22; TRIP/H Rogers p13; Skip Novak PPL p7; Zefa/Damm p6; Zefa/Kurt Goebel p20; Zefa/G Mabbs p21.

Cover photograph by Trevor Clifford.
Commissioned photography arranged by Hilary Fletcher.

Thanks to David Byrne for his comments on the initial draft.

The Publishers would like to thank Toys R Us Ltd The Worlds Biggest Toy Megastore, NES Arnold Ltd, Do It All Ltd, F. Hinds and Halfords for the kind loan of equipment and material used in this book.

Every effort has been made to contact copyright holders of any material reproduced in this book. Any omissions will be rectified in subsequent printings if notice is given to the Publisher.

Contents

What are pulleys and gears?

Pulleys and gears are special wheels. They help to make some machines move.

When you turn the crank handle on this model windmill, it makes the sails turn too. The handle and the sails are linked by a rubber band. This is the **drive belt**. The drive belt is stretched over two pulleys. It makes both pulleys turn together.

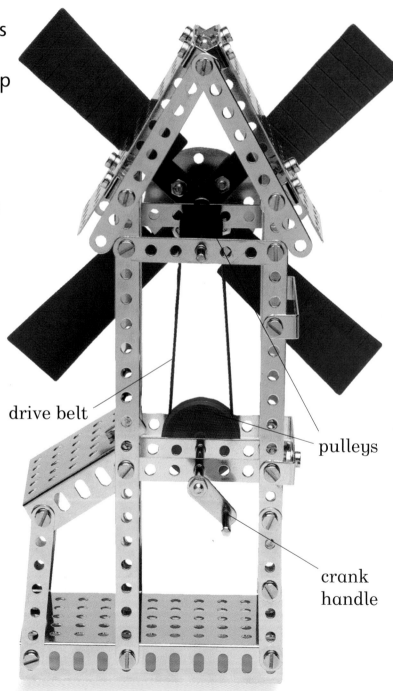

drive belt

pulleys

crank handle

The crank handle of this model is linked to the wheels by two gear wheels. The gear wheels have teeth around their edges. Some of the teeth on one wheel fit between some of the teeth on the other wheel. This is called **meshing**.

gear wheels

crank handle

When one gear wheel turns, its teeth push the teeth on the other gear wheel. This makes the second gear wheel turn as well.

Different directions

When two pulleys are linked by a drive belt they go round in the same direction. Two gear wheels with meshed teeth go round in opposite directions.

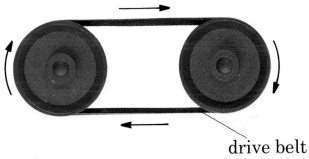

drive belt

Up the pole

To make a flag go up a pole you pull down on the rope. As you pull down the flag goes up. How can a pull down make something go up?

If you look at the top of the pole you will see the answer. The rope goes over a pulley. The pulley changes the direction of the pull from down to up. So, as you pull down on the rope, the flag goes up.

Can you spot the pulleys on this yacht? Pulleys help sailors to raise the sails up the mast. The sailors pull down on ropes on the deck.

FACT

The first pulleys

Who invented the pulley? No one knows, but the first pulleys were probably just smooth tree branches. Many people must have had the idea of throwing a rope over a tree branch to lift a heavy load high enough to keep it out of the reach of animals, or to put it on a cart.

FILE

Cranes and block and tackle

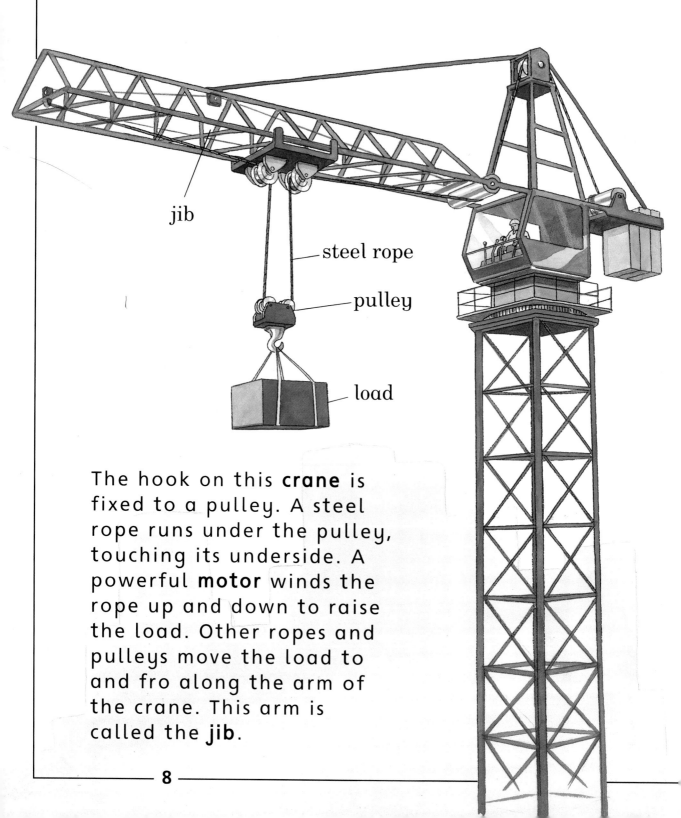

jib

steel rope

pulley

load

The hook on this **crane** is fixed to a pulley. A steel rope runs under the pulley, touching its underside. A powerful **motor** winds the rope up and down to raise the load. Other ropes and pulleys move the load to and fro along the arm of the crane. This arm is called the **jib**.

A block and tackle is a set of pulleys that work together. One person can lift a very heavy weight with a block and tackle. This boat was lifted out of the sea using the block and tackle.

Making it easy

With two pulleys you can lift twice as much weight with the same amount of pull. With more pulleys you can lift even heavier loads.

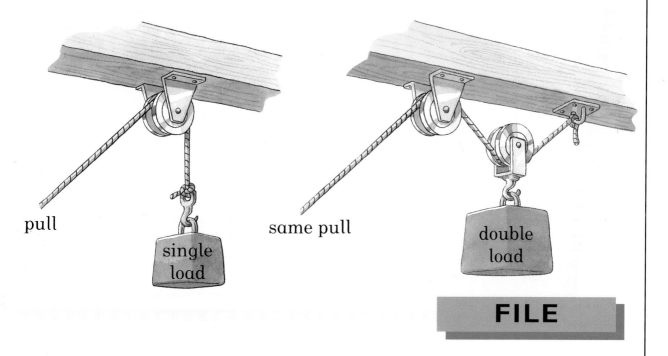

pull

single load

same pull

double load

Drive belts

A **steam engine** drives this old-fashioned sewing machine. The engine is joined to the sewing machine by pulleys and a **drive belt**. The pulley on the machine is smaller than the pulley on the engine. This makes the sewing machine turn faster than the engine.

These pulley wheels are linked by a drive belt. Two wheels of the same size turn at the same speed.

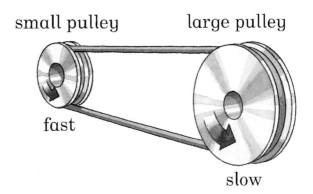

same size – same speed

When the wheels are different sizes, the smaller wheel turns faster than the bigger one.

small pulley   large pulley

fast

slow

You can make pulley wheels turn in opposite directions by twisting and crossing over the drive belt.

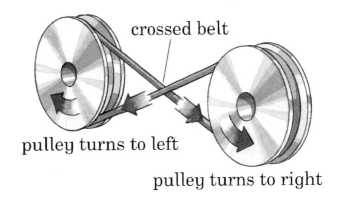

crossed belt

pulley turns to left

pulley turns to right

FACT

Half the size, twice the speed

If one pulley is half the size of the other pulley, it turns round twice as quickly. This is because one turn of the large pulley makes the small pulley go round twice.

FILE

Power pulleys

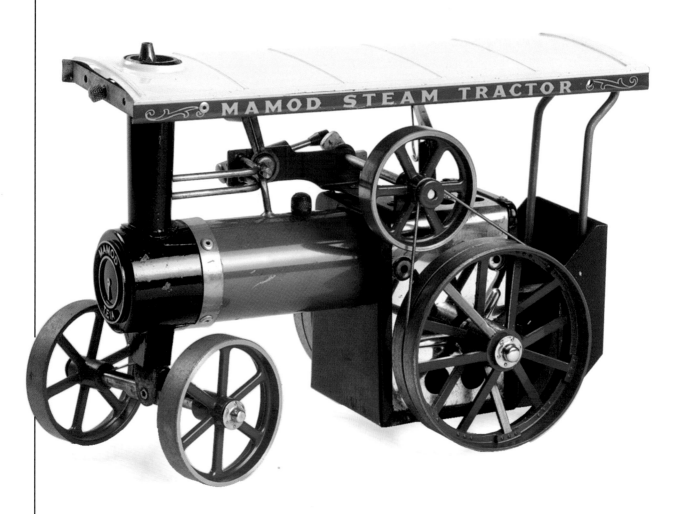

Most of the rides at the fairground go round and round. Some of them were worked by **steam engines** with pulleys and drive belts. This is a model of an old steam engine. It has a **drive belt** that turns the back wheel to drive the engine along.

This machine crushes sugar cane to extract the juice. It has many moving parts. A steam engine drives it. Drive belts, pulleys and gears make the parts go round.

Gear kits

You can learn about gears by making models with a gear kit. Flat, round gears are called **spur gears**. One spur gear can turn several other gears. This is called a **gear train**. The gears in the train go round in different directions. If the gears are different sizes, they go round at different speeds.

A gear wheel which looks like a screw is called a worm gear. When a **worm gear** turns it makes a large spur gear go round very slowly.

Two gear wheels can be linked together with a chain that fits over their teeth. This is how the gears on a bicycle work. The chain makes both gear wheels go round in the same direction.

Count the teeth

These three gear wheels have 7 teeth, 10 teeth and 14 teeth. Which two gears would you choose to make one gear turn twice as fast as the other? Look at page 24 to see if you were right.

Drills, whisks and reels

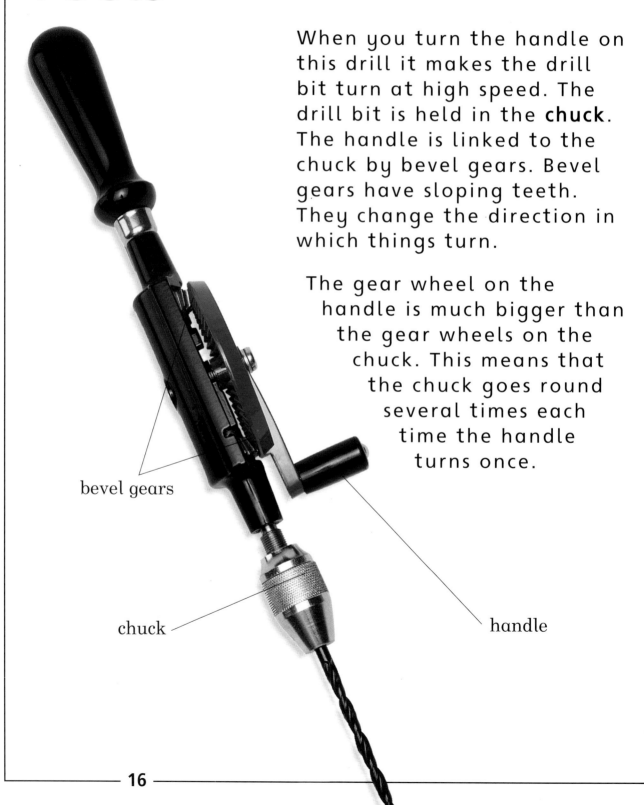

When you turn the handle on this drill it makes the drill bit turn at high speed. The drill bit is held in the **chuck**. The handle is linked to the chuck by bevel gears. Bevel gears have sloping teeth. They change the direction in which things turn.

The gear wheel on the handle is much bigger than the gear wheels on the chuck. This means that the chuck goes round several times each time the handle turns once.

bevel gears

chuck

handle

This whisk has two blades. They are turned by gear wheels on either side of the big gear wheel on the handle. The blades turn in opposite directions, so everything mixes in very well.

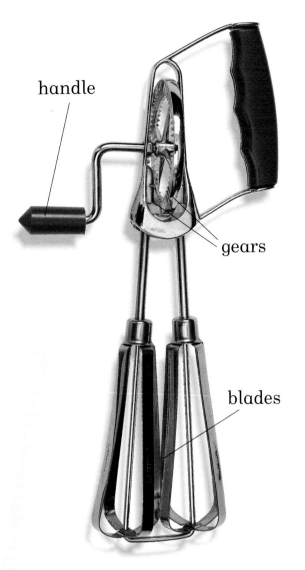

handle

gears

blades

Changing direction

Gear wheels inside this fishing reel change the direction of the turn on the handle. As the handle turns it winds in the line.

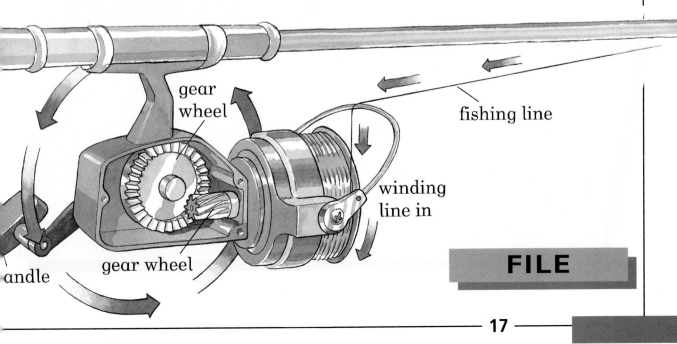

gear wheel

fishing line

winding line in

gear wheel

handle

Clocks and watches

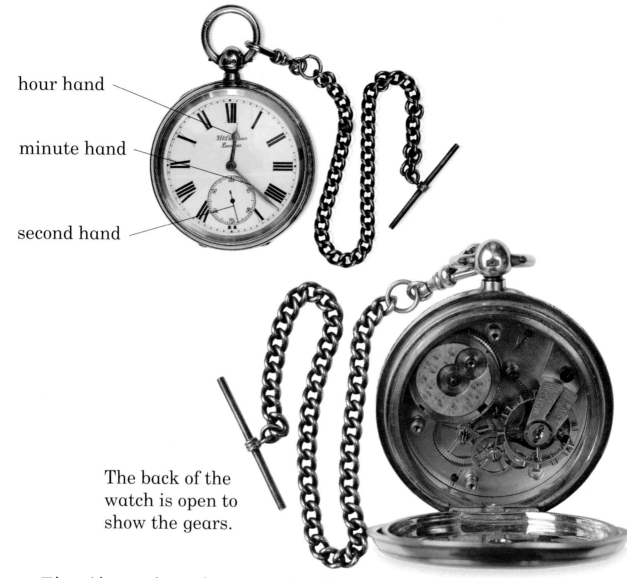

hour hand

minute hand

second hand

The back of the watch is open to show the gears.

The three hands on a clock or watch go round at different speeds. The same **mechanism** turns them all. Each hand is linked to the mechanism by different gears.

During the time the hour hand turns one complete circle, the minute hand turns 12 times. Extra gears help the hour hand go more slowly than the minute hand.

Gears turn the hands of a cuckoo clock. They are powered by falling weights instead of a **motor**. Extra gears turn the parts that make the cuckoo pop out every hour.

Time flies!

The hour hand on a clock goes all the way round twice in 24 hours. The minute hand goes round 24 times, but the second hand goes round 1440 times every 24 hours!

Mills

gears

grindstone

Huge gear wheels turn round
inside a windmill. They carry
the turning force of the sails to
the **grindstones**. This is how
wheat and other grains were
ground into flour. Some gears in
old mills are made from wood.

The gear wheels in this water-mill are made from metal. Metal gears are stronger and last longer than wooden gears. They must be greased to make them run smoothly.

The gear wheels in this toy mill are made from plastic. Plastic gears turn smoothly without grease. They are not as strong as metal ones.

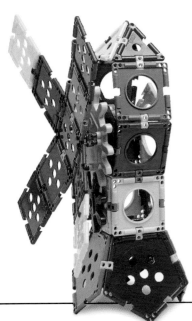

Mountain bikes

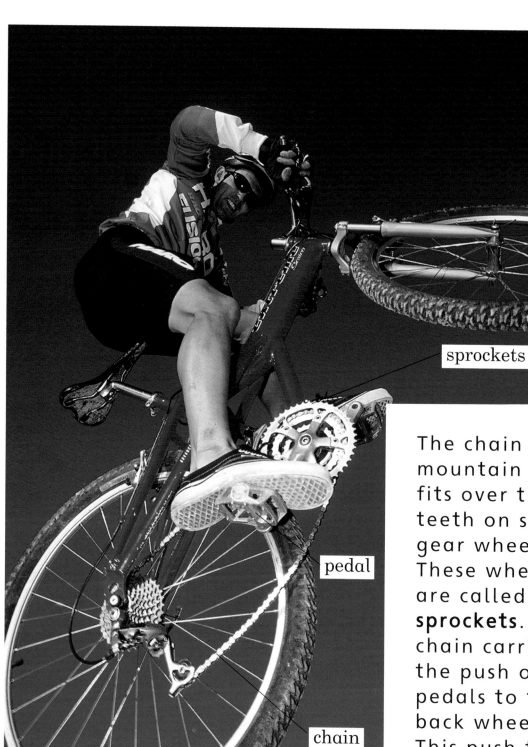

sprockets

pedal

chain

The chain on a mountain bike fits over the teeth on special gear wheels. These wheels are called **sprockets**. The chain carries the push on the pedals to the back wheel. This push turns the back wheel.

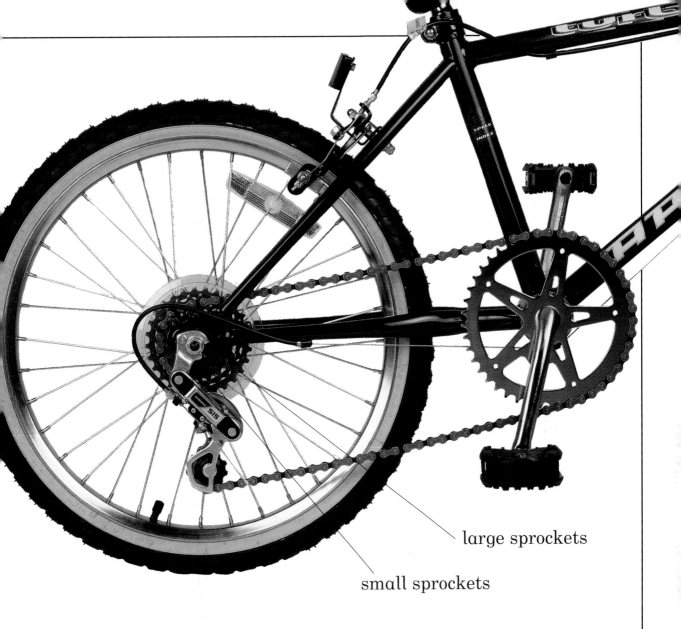

large sprockets

small sprockets

When you change gear on a bike, the chain moves between different sized sprockets on the back wheel. Large sprockets are easy gears for climbing hills. Small sprockets are hard gears for going fast along flat ground.

FACT

How many gears?

Some mountain bikes have 28 gears! Track racing bikes have only one gear.

FILE

Glossary

chuck The part on a drill that grips the different sized drill bits.

drive belt A loop of leather or rubber that links one pulley wheel to another.

gear train A series of gear wheels which carry turning movements from one part of a machine to another.

grindstone A wheel made from stone which is used to sharpen tools and smooth rough metal.

jib The long arm on a crane.

mechanism The parts, such as pulleys and gears, which move together to make a machine work.

mesh When the teeth on two gear wheels fit together

motor A machine that uses electricity or fuels such as petrol or coal to make things move.

sprockets The toothed wheels on the pedals and back wheel of a bicycle.

spur gear Flat circular gears with teeth around the edge.

steam engine A motor or engine which uses steam from boiling water to make things move.

worm gear A gear like a screw with a spiral thread running around its surface.

Index

The answer to the question on page 15 is –
the 7-toothed wheel goes twice as fast as the 14-toothed wheel.
Were you right?

SIMPLE MACHINES

By • DEBORAH • HODGE

PHOTOGRAPHS BY RAY BOUDREAU

Heinemann Children's Reference and Kids Can Press Ltd acknowledge
with appreciation the assistance of the Canada Council, the Ontario
Arts Council and Gavin Barrett in the production of this book.

First published in Canada in 1996 by Kids Can Press Ltd,
29 Birch Avenue, Toronto, Ontario, Canada, M4V 1E2.
This edition published in Great Britain in 1997 by
Heinemann Children's Reference, an imprint of Heinemann
Educational Publishers, Halley Court, Jordan Hill, Oxford, OX2 8EJ.

MADRID ATHENS PARIS FLORENCE PORTSMOUTH NH
CHICAGO SAO PAULO SINGAPORE TOKYO MELBOURNE
AUCKLAND IBADAN GABORONE JOHANNESBURG
KAMPALA NAIROBI

Text copyright © 1996 by Deborah Hodge
Photographs copyright © 1996 by Ray Boudreau

British Library Cataloguing in Publication Data
A catalogue record for this book is available from the
British Library.

ISBN 0 431 01614 3 (hardback) 0 431 01619 4 (paperback)

PLEASE READ THIS
For some of the activities in this book you will need to use
tools and materials such as scissors or a knife. Be very
careful when you are using them, and always make sure an
adult is there to help you. Don't eat raw eggs, and wash your
hands when you have done the activity on pages 18-19.

Edited by Valerie Wyatt and Alex Gray.
Designed by James Ireland.
Printed in Hong Kong.

Table of contents

Table trick

Can you lift a friend without touching them? You can with the help of a simple machine called a lever. **Warning:** This test is for older children only, and should be supervised by an adult.

You will need:
- a small table
- a sturdy straight-backed chair
- a strong broomstick

What to do:
1. Ask a friend to sit or lie on the table near one edge and hold on. Grab on to the edge of the table and try to lift it and your friend. Is this hard to do?

2. Put the chair near the table with its seat facing away.

3. Lay the broomstick over the chair back. Wedge one end of the stick under the table top.

4. Put one knee on the chair seat to hold it down. Slowly push down on the free end of the broomstick. What happens?

5. Try moving the chair closer or farther from the table. Is lifting the table easier or harder?

What's happening?
When you push down on one end of the broomstick, your pushing power is changed into a strong lifting power at the other end.

A lever
The broomstick is working as a lever — a type of simple machine. A lever is any stiff bar that turns on a resting point called a fulcrum. (In this case, the fulcrum is the back of the chair.) The lever helps you lift heavy things by turning your pushing force into a smaller but more powerful lifting movement.

Simple machines
A lever is one of six simple machines. The others are: the wheel and axle, the pulley, the inclined plane, the screw and the wedge. Simple machines don't need engines to work — only the power of your muscles. Simple machines make tough jobs easier by changing the power, speed or direction of a movement.

Balancing act

Have you ever played on a see-saw? Here's a trick that will show you how to lift two friends all by yourself.

You will need:
- scissors
- the cardboard tube from a roll of kitchen paper
- a ruler
- some building blocks or coins

What to do:
1. Younger children should ask an adult to cut the cardboard tube in half, lengthwise. Place one piece on a table, with the cut part down.

2. Set the ruler on top. Put a block on each end of the ruler. Can you make them balance?

3. Pile more blocks on one end of the ruler. How many blocks can you lift with just one block on the other end? **Hint:** You will need to move the tube closer to the pile of blocks or the blocks closer to the tube.

What's happening?
Your ruler is working as a lever. The longer the distance between the single block and the cardboard tube (the fulcrum), the more blocks you can lift. To lift two friends on a see-saw (which is also a lever), sit a long way from the fulcrum (the middle) and have your friends sit near it.

Wacky wheels

If you have taken a ride on a bike, you'll know that wheels help you go places. How? Make this toy car and find out.

You will need:

- an empty cardboard milk carton, 1 litre size
- scissors
- a long smooth board
- some thick books
- 2 long pencil crayons sharpened at both ends
- 4 large cotton reels

What to do:

1. Ask an adult to cut the milk carton in half lengthwise, to make two car bodies.
2. Raise one end of the board on a pile of books. Place one car, without wheels, at the top of the ramp. What happens?
3. Ask an adult to use the scissors to poke holes at the front and back of the other car. Each hole should be about the size of a penny.

4. Slide a pencil crayon through the front holes. Slide another pencil crayon through the back holes.
5. Push a reel onto the end of each pencil crayon. Leave a small space between the reel and the side of the car. The reel must be able to turn.
6. Put the car at the top of the ramp again and let it go.

What's happening?

Without wheels, your car can't move. There's too much friction (rubbing) between it and the ground. Wheels reduce the amount of friction so that your car can zoom down the ramp.

A wheel and axle

When you combine a wheel (the spool) with an axle (the pencil crayon), you have a simple machine called a wheel and axle. You can move heavy objects by putting a wheel and axle under them.

Sweet collector

Can you lift a sweet just by blowing?

You will need:

- scissors
- a piece of coloured sugar paper
- a pencil and ruler
- tape
- a long pencil crayon
- an empty cardboard milk carton
- a piece of string 30 cm long
- a sweet with a hole in it

What to do:

1. Younger children should ask an adult to cut out a square piece of sugar paper 18 x 18 cm and mark it as shown.

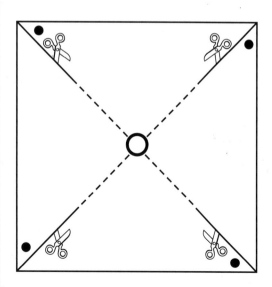

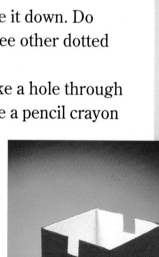

2. Starting at one corner, cut halfway down the pencil line. Do the same for the other corners.

3. Fold one dotted corner point over so that it just touches the centre circle. Tape it down. Do the same with the three other dotted corner points.

4. Ask an adult to poke a hole through the centre circle. Slide a pencil crayon through the hole.

5. Cut off the top of the milk carton and cut two slots as shown.

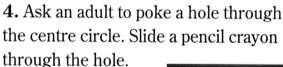

6. Tie one end of the string to the sweet. Tie the other end to the pencil crayon and tape it in place. Set the pencil in the milk carton slots.

7. Hold on to the base of the windmill and blow on the sails. Can you make them turn? What happens to the sweet?

What's happening?

Your windmill is a wheel and axle machine. The paper wheel and pencil axle change the forward movement of your breath into a turning movement. The turning causes the string to wind up and lift the sweet.

Bubble race

Challenge a friend to see who can whip up the biggest batch of bubbles in the shortest time.

You will need:

- 2 mixing bowls of the same size
- washing up liquid
- a teaspoon
- a mixing spoon
- a rotary eggbeater
- a clock or watch that shows seconds

What to do:

1. Half fill each bowl with water.

2. Pour a teaspoon of washing up liquid into each bowl. Do not stir.

3. Give your friend the mixing spoon. You will use the eggbeater. Starting at the same time, use your mixing tools to whip up the soap and water. Mix as fast as you can for 30 seconds. Who makes the most bubbles?

What's happening?

The eggbeater is a wheel and axle machine. It is made up of wheels that work together, called gears. When you turn the handle, a large wheel moves smaller gear wheels. As the small gears turn, they make the beaters spin fast. The gears are changing your hand movement into a faster motion. This helps you whip up the most bubbles in the shortest time.

Gears

Gears are wheels with teeth that turn and work together. The size of the gears and the way they work together can give you more speed or power. A large gear turning smaller ones will give more speed. A small gear turning large ones will give you more power.

Going up!

What do you call a wheel that turns on a rope and lifts heavy weights? A pulley. How does it work? Make this toy lift and see.

You will need:

- a piece of string 60 cm long
- a small empty cotton reel
- tape
- some heavy books
- 1 m of ribbon (wide enough to fit snugly between the rims of the cotton reel)
- a small plastic bucket
- small objects to lift

What to do:

1. Thread the string through the centre hole of the cotton reel.
2. Tape the ends of the string to a table top so that the reel hangs about 10 cm below the table's edge. Use the heavy books to hold the ends of the string in place.
3. Tie one end of the ribbon to the handle of the bucket.
4. Slide the free end of the ribbon over the cotton reel. Slowly pull down on the free end. What happens to the bucket?
5. Place small objects in your bucket lift. Try lifting them.

What's happening?

When you pull *down* on the ribbon, the bucket is lifted *up*. The direction of the force you are using to pull is transferred into a force that lifts.

A pulley

When you combine a wheel (in this case, the reel) with a rope (the ribbon), you have a pulley. A pulley can change the direction of the force exerted by your muscles. Instead of lifting a heavy object straight up, you pull down on a rope attached to it. Pulling down is

Pulling power

Invite your friends to a pulling contest and surprise them with your strength.

You will need:
- a piece of rope about 3 m long
- 2 broomsticks

What to do:
1. Knot one end of the rope to the end of a broomstick.

2. Ask your friends to stand facing each other about 30 cm apart. Give them each a broomstick. Tell them to hold the broomsticks parallel — the same distance apart at both ends.

3. Loop the rope around the broomsticks as shown in the picture.

4. Challenge your friends to hold the broomsticks apart while you pull *steadily* on the free end of the rope. Who wins?

What's happening?
The chances are you were able to pull the broomsticks together. Why? The rope and broomsticks act as a movable pulley. This pulley increases the force you use, giving you extra pulling power.

When you're ready to try this trick, lift the sticks off the floor.

17

Egg drop

Ever wanted to drop an egg and watch what happens? Here's your chance!

You will need:

- 2 eggs. Use hard-boiled eggs if you want to reduce the risk of breaking the eggs.
- 2 food tins, about 8 cm tall
- scissors
- an empty foil box or similar box
- tape

What to do:

1. Hold an egg in one hand. Rest the hand on top of a tin as the boy is doing in the picture. Let the egg drop. Does it crack?
2. Cut off the lid and one end of the box.
3. Make a ramp by taping the closed end of the box to the top of one tin.
4. Place an egg at the top of the ramp and let it roll down. When the egg stops, check it.

What's happening?

The force of the egg being dropped and hitting the plate was so great that the shell cracked. When the egg rolled down the ramp, the force was less — not enough to crack it. The difference was the ramp. This is a simple machine with an inclined plane (sloping surface).

An inclined plane

An inclined plane allows you to lower (or lift) heavy objects using less force. But to use less force you must move the object over a longer distance. Measure the length of the ramp. Now measure the height of the tin. Which way does the egg have to travel further — when it's dropped straight down or when it's rolled gently along the ramp?

Penny lift

Have you ever run up a ramp? If so, you were using a simple machine with an inclined plane (sloping surface). Here's how to put an inclined plane to work.

You will need:

- some books
- a board or book at least 35 cm long
- a knife
- a small plastic yogurt container
- a piece of string three times as long as the board
- a toy car
- 20 or more marbles or small coins

What to do:

1. Put a small pile of books near the edge of a table. Rest one edge of the board on top. This is your inclined plane, a ramp.
2. Ask an adult to poke two small holes near the top of the yogurt container, on opposite sides. Thread the string through the holes and tie it as shown.

3. Tie or tape the other end of the string to the toy car.
4. Set the car near the bottom of the ramp. Drape the string up over the board, so that the yogurt container hangs just over the edge of the board, as shown on the right.
5. Place marbles or small coins, one at a time, into the container until the car moves to the top of the ramp. How many marbles or coins does it take?
6. Make a steeper ramp by placing a taller stack of books under the board. Does it take more marbles or coins to move the car to the top, or fewer?

What's happening?

The weight of the marbles or coins is the force that makes the car move. The steeper the inclined plane (the ramp), the larger the force (marbles or coins) you must use.

Screwy water

Most water flows downhill. But not the water in this picture. It's flowing up! Try it yourself with the help of a simple machine.

You will need:

- a piece of plastic tubing 135 cm long
- tape
- a tall, empty cardboard tube or tin
- a mixing bowl
- food colouring

What to do:

1. Tape one end of the plastic tubing to the top of the tin. Wind the tubing around the tin in a spiral. The tubing should look like turns on a screw. Tape the end to the bottom of the tin.

2. Three-quarters fill the bowl with water. Then mix in a few drops of food colouring.

3. Place the top end of the tin and tubing into the bowl. Slowly turn the tin until coloured water moves into the tubing.

4. Lift the tin out of the bowl and tilt it slightly.

5. Slowly turn the tin and watch what happens. If the water doesn't climb, try holding the tin at a slightly different angle.

What's happening?

The spiral tubing makes it easier for the water to climb up. The tubing acts as a screw — a simple machine used to fasten and to lift or move things.

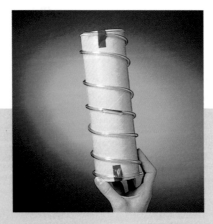

A screw

A screw has grooves that wind around to form a gentle slope. The slope is like an inclined plane — it lets you move things using less force. By winding around, a screw (the tubing, in this case) makes a longer but more gentle slope for the water to move up.

23

Twirling toy

Make this toy helicopter and watch it fly. It's actually a simple machine that makes a soft landing every time.

You will need:

- a piece of paper 18 x 5 cm
- a piece of tracing paper
- a pencil
- scissors
- a paper clip

What to do:

1. Trace the pattern below onto the piece of paper. Make sure you use solid and dotted lines in the correct place.

2. Cut the solid lines A and B. Younger children should ask an adult to cut the solid lines. Fold along the dotted lines C and D. Fold along the dotted line E.

3. Slide a paper clip onto the folded tip.

4. Cut the solid line F. Bend flap G back and flap H forward.

5. Lift your toy helicopter up high and let it go. How does it move? Try flying it from a higher spot.

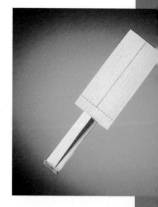

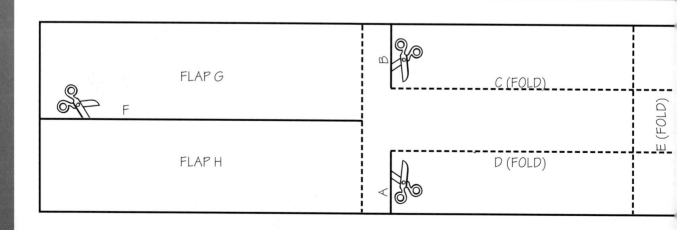

What's happening?

Your toy helicopter twirls in a spiral as it drops. The twirling blades act as a screw — a simple machine that helps you lift or lower things with less force. Turning in a spiral allows the helicopter to drop with less force, so it flies down more slowly. It lands softly instead of crashing down.

25

Funny face

Make a funny fruit face. A simple machine will help you do it.

You will need:
- a paring knife
- a carrot
- an apple (choose a soft type)

What to do:
1. Ask an adult to slice the carrot. First cut it into circles about 0.5 cm thick.
2. Try pushing one carrot circle into the apple. What happens?
3. Cut another carrot circle into a point.

4. Push the point of the carrot into the apple. Which shape of carrot is easier to push in — the point or circle?
5. Cut the other carrot circles into points. Push them into the apple to make a funny face. Try other fruits and vegetables to make more funny creatures.

What's happening?
It's easier to push in the pointed piece of carrot because it acts as a wedge — a simple device used to fix and to separate or split things.

26

A wedge

A wedge is thick at one end and thin at the other. It is used to force things apart or fix things tightly. When you push at the wide end of the carrot wedge, the thin end goes into the apple first. As you push further, the thicker part pushes against the sides of the apple. The wedge pushes the apple's insides further and further apart.

Mystery machine

Are you in the mood to solve a mystery? Make this toy paddle boat to float in a bathtub or paddling pool. While you're at it, try to figure out which two simple machines help the boat move.

You will need:

- scissors
- a clean, empty cardboard milk carton 1 litre size
- 2 pencils
- 2 small elastic bands

What to do:

1. Ask an adult to cut the carton in half lengthwise. Use one half for the body of your boat.

2. Ask an adult to poke two holes in the flat end of the carton. Slide a pencil into each hole, leaving the ends sticking out about 7 cm.

3. Cut a piece 7 cm x 3 cm out of the other half of the carton. This piece is the paddle for your boat.

4. Put one elastic band around the pencil ends inside the body of the boat. The elastic will be loose.

5. Put the other elastic band around the pencil ends sticking out of the boat. Slip the paddle between this elastic band and wind it up about 25 times.

6. Holding on to the paddle, place the boat in a bathtub of water. Let it go and watch it paddle around.

Hint: If the boat goes backwards, you should wind the paddle in the other direction.

What's happening?

Two simple machines are helping the boat go. At the front of the boat is a wedge. Can you see the wide part that narrows into a point? This is called the bow. A wedge-shaped bow helps a boat cut through the water. At the back of the boat, the paddle is a wheel turning on an elastic-band axle. As the paddle turns, it pushes or pulls the boat through the water.

For parents and teachers

The activities in this book are designed to teach children about six simple machines: the lever, wheel and axle, pulley, inclined plane, screw and wedge. Simple machines do not save work, but they make tough jobs (such as lifting heavy objects) easier by changing the power, speed or direction of a force. Here are some ideas to extend the activities in the book.

Table trick

What else is a lever? Look for a bottle opener, shovel, crowbar, stapler, drinks can tab, claw end of a hammer, pair of scissors, nutcrackers, tweezers or pliers. To see how these levers make work easier, try doing the same work without them.

Balancing act

How many more blocks can be lifted by increasing the distance between the fulcrum and the single block? Repeat the experiment using a longer ruler.

Wacky wheels

Ask a child to sit on an upside-down trolley, then try to pull it. Turn the trolley upright and try again. Which way is easier? Sliding friction (without wheels) is greater than rolling friction (with wheels).

Sweet collector

In a real windmill, the wind turns blades that revolve on an axle. The turning axle causes gears and other machine parts to move and do useful work, such as pumping water or grinding grain. How much weight can the sweet collector lift? Try adding more sweets.

Bubble race

Working together, gears can change the power, speed or direction of a movement. How do gears on a bicycle work? Turn a bicycle upside down, turn the pedals and watch the gears as you try a low gear, then higher gears. Try riding uphill and on level ground in different gears. Which gears work best for each?

Going up!

Have a pulley hunt. Look for pulleys on a clothes line, flag pole, crane, sailing boat or fishing boat. What is each pulley being used to move?

Pulling power

Use a longer rope and make a few more loops around the broomsticks. Does this make it easier to pull the sticks together? (The more turns of the rope, the easier it is. But for every turn, the distance you have to pull the rope is increased.)

Egg drop and Penny lift

Try 'Egg drop' using a steeper ramp. Does the egg have a harder or softer landing? Try 'Penny lift' using a longer ramp. Does it take more or less force (more or fewer coins) to move a car up a longer ramp? Look for other ramps that people use.

Screwy water and Twirling toy

A screw can help you lift or lower things with less force, but it also has another important use — as a strong fastener. Have a hunt to find screws used as fasteners. Look for a wood screw, corkscrew, coat hook, large hook-style plant hanger, the vice on a workbench, toothpaste tube cap and screw-on jar lid. What is each screw holding in place?

Funny face

Bite into an apple with your front teeth. Take another bite with your back teeth. Which teeth are sharper biters? (Your front teeth — because they are wedges.) What else is a wedge? A toothpick, pin, sewing needle, nail, axe, chisel, knife and scissor blades.

Mystery machine

Most machines are made up of two or more simple machines. Try inventing your own mystery machine by combining some simple machines. What work can you get your mystery machine to do?

Words to know

axle: a bar or rod that a wheel turns on

force: a push or pull on an object that causes it to move, stop or change direction. A force can make an object move faster or slower.

friction: the rubbing force of one object against another. Friction causes moving objects to slow down.

fulcrum: the resting or balance point upon which a lever turns

gear: a wheel with ridges or teeth. One gear connects and turns another.

inclined plane: a sloping surface used to move loads up or down

lever: a stiff bar that turns on a fulcrum and is used to move heavy loads

pulley: a wheel with a groove that a rope or wire fits into. A pulley is used to lift or move things.

ramp: an inclined plane

screw: a sloping surface that winds in a spiral around a shaft. A screw is used to fasten or move things.

simple machine: a machine that operates without an engine and is used to make work easier. A simple machine changes the power, speed or direction of a movement.

wedge: an object with a wide end and a pointed or sharp end. A wedge is used to split or separate things, or to fix them in position.

wheel and axle: a wheel or set of wheels fastened to a bar or rod. A wheel and axle is used to move things or change the power, speed or direction of a movement.

Index